Learn to Cook

Soups

Learn to Cook

Soups

Janet Marsh Lillie

HARLAXTON

Page two: Roast Pumpkin Soup with Saffron Threads (p. 47)—the success of this delicious dish is guaranteed if you roast the entire pumpkin one day ahead. The preparation is shown on the endpapers.

Published by
Harlaxton Publishing Limited
2 Avenue Road, Grantham, Lincolnshire, NG31 6TA
United Kingdom
A Member of the Weldon International Group of Companies

First Published in 1994

© Copyright 1994 Harlaxton Publishing Limited
© Copyright 1994 Design Harlaxton Publishing Limited

Publisher: Robin Burgess
Project Coordinator: Barbara Beckett
Designer: Rachel Rush
Editor: Alison Leach
Illustrator: Maggie Renvoize
Jacket photographer: Rodney Weidland
Inside photography: Jack Sarafian
Food stylist: Janet Marsh Lillie
Produced by Barbara Beckett Publishing
Colour Separation: G.A. Graphics, Stamford, UK
Printer: Imago, Singapore

British Library Cataloguing-in-Publication data.
A catalogue record for this book is available from the British Library

Title: Learn to Cook, SOUPS
ISBN: 1 85837 077 9

Contents

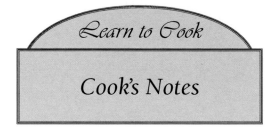

Cook's Notes

Measurements

All spoon and cup measurements are level. Standard spoon and cup measures are used in all the recipes. I recommend using a graduated nest of measuring cups: 1 cup, ½ cup, ⅓rd cup and ¼ cup. The graduated nest of spoons comprises 1 tablespoon, 1 teaspoon, ½ teaspoon and ¼ teaspoon. For liquids, use a standard litre or imperial pint measuring jug, which also shows cup measurements. As the metric/imperial/US equivalents given are not exact, follow only one system of measurement within the recipe.

Ovens should be preheated to the specified temperature. When cooking in a saucepan or frying pan (skillet), use a moderate heat unless directed otherwise.

Fresh vegetables and fruits are medium size unless otherwise stated. In soup making, the weights are not critical; a gram or ounce or two under or over will not affect your final results. The weights reflect the produce before it is prepared for cooking.

Ingredients

Fresh ingredients are used in the recipes unless otherwise stated. **Canned products**, in particular tomatoes, corn kernels, tuna and a variety of pulses such as red kidney beans, are used not only to save time in preparation but because they are excellent convenience products. If the weight listed is not the same as that available to you, buy the nearest equivalent.

Most of the recipes rely on chicken, beef or fish stock to add the flavour base to each soup. However, if you are unable to make your own stock, look for canned equivalents recognized as broths or consommés. Alternatively, you can use stock cubes or powders. The powders recommend 1 teaspoon per 250 ml/8 fl oz/1 cup water, but they will vary in strength, so I suggest using 3 teaspoons of the particular flavour base per litre/1¾ pints/4¼ cups of water.

Herb quantities are for fresh herbs; if fresh are not available, use half the quantity of dried herbs. Use freshly ground black **pepper** whenever pepper is listed; use **salt** and pepper to individual taste. Use plain (all-purpose) **flour** unless otherwise stated. Use olive or vegetable **oils**. Choose a medium to good quality **wine** if this ingredient is used — cheap varieties do not enhance the final flavour.

Tomato Pepper Ice (p. 30)—munchy, crunchy, spicy and icy this is the simplified version of the tasty and tangy Gazpacho soup.

Introduction

Soup, glorious soup — there is nothing more delicious and comforting in the depths of winter than a steaming, aromatic bowl of soup or, in contrast, a chilled creation for a summer's day. Soups served as everyday family meals or as a beginning to a stylish or impromptu menu offer a wide variety of colour and flavour. This book will provide both everyday and innovative combinations for you to enjoy.

Basically, soups fall into the categories of thin or thick. An important element in their making is the liquid in which the ingredients are simmered. Some soups need only water, because ingredients such as spinach, asparagus, cucumber and some pulses create their own flavours which are a highlight in the final result. However, a cooking liquid known as stock is essential to the success of other soups such as clear broths and concentrated or double consommés, and cream, purée and thick soups.

Recipes for these basic stocks — beef, chicken and fish — are given on pages 11–12. There are no rigid rules for making stocks. The recipes list suggested ingredients; you can add extra ingredients such as washed fresh vegetable peelings and beef or chicken bones to concentrate their flavours. Once you have made a good, well-flavoured stock, it can be frozen and kept for up to six months. Store it in plastic containers, labelled and dated, in handy amounts — 600 ml/1 pint/2 ½ cups or larger. It may also be stored in ice-cube trays. In this way you will have stock on hand not only for soups but for sauces and casseroles too.

Under each of the soup categories there is a selection of recipes that illustrate the technique and introduce you to exciting and subtle flavours, with suggestions for simple garnishes and accompaniments. Step-by-step guides to procedures such as puréeing, thickening soups with different liaisons, removing fat from a stock and straining a consommé are included. There are also handy tips to help you with preparation techniques you may not be familiar with — how to skin and remove the seeds from tomatoes, how to peel garlic, how to prepare croûtons, to mention a few.

A glossary of cooking terms appears on page 47 for you to look up any term that is unfamiliar. There is a list of recipes on page 5 for your reference. Be sure to read the information on measurements and ingredients on page 6.

An important thing to do when trying a new recipe is to read the recipe thoroughly before starting, so that you understand the method and have the ingredients required and the necessary equipment. For soup making the equipment needed is: a chopping board, sharp knives in different sizes, a vegetable peeler, tongs, a wire whisk, large sieves (strainers) for puréeing or straining, heavy-based saucepans with lids — at least one saucepan that will hold 3 litres/ 5¼ pints/3½ quarts — paper towels, wooden spoons and, of course, soup bowls for serving.

A blender or food processor is another worthwhile piece of equipment, because both cream and purée soups rely on blending cooked ingredients to create the base in to which the finishing

Chopping Spring Onions (Scallions) and Slicing Chicken

Cut the root end off spring onion and trim the top. *Chop the spring onion finely on the diagonal.* *Cut the chicken into manageable portions.* *Cut these portions into fine strips.*

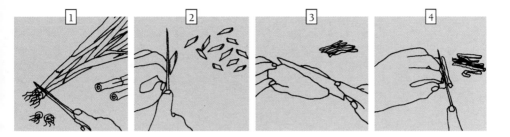

touches are stirred or whisked and the garnish added. If you do not already have one as part of your kitchen, it is a good investment, saving time and energy because it performs so many other valuable jobs like chopping nuts and fresh herbs and blending sauces and mayonnaise.

The soup recipes that follow cover the well-known, the traditional and the unusual. I hope you enjoy preparing them as much as I have enjoyed compiling them.

Preparation of vegetables for Watercress Vegetable Soup (p. 16)—a helpful hint is to prepare all of the vegetables well ahead of time.

Clear Soups

There is nothing like a piping hot, appetizing clear soup to stimulate the palate. The essential base, the stock, is prepared very easily from simple, everyday ingredients. If you already have some stock stored in the refrigerator, frozen as small blocks or sealed in labelled plastic containers, you can turn it into a nourishing soup in minutes by adding seasonings like sambal olek (a paste made from chillies) such as 1–2 teaspoons of soy sauce per person, a dash of tomato paste, finely chopped fresh herbs, red pepper (capsicum, bell pepper), spring onions (scallions) or a dash of lemon juice, sherry or brandy.

The ingredients for stocks as suggested are flexible. You may have a simple recipe you prefer. However, there are some tips you should know about before you begin:

Always use fresh, good quality meat, bones and vegetables.

Bones from roast joints, poultry, meat and vegetables scraps can be added to intensify the stock's flavour.

Avoid using potato and parsnip, as these will cloud the stock. Cabbage will give an 'off' flavour.

Avoid using fat.

Avoid boiling the stock, as it can become cloudy. Instead, simmer for the suggested time; the surface of the liquid should move only slightly.

Preparation of Beef Stock—it's elementary!
The essential technique is to brown the beef bones before adding the water.

Beef Stock

SUGGESTED INGREDIENTS

3 tablespoons oil
1.5 kg/3¼ lb beef bones
375 g/13 oz or more of shin beef
3 litres/5¼ pints/3½ quarts cold water
2 celery sticks, chopped

2–3 carrots, roughly chopped
2 brown onions, including skins, roughly chopped
2 tomatoes, cut in half
Thyme and a bay leaf

Heat 2 tablespoons of the oil in a stockpot or large saucepan and brown the bones and shin beef until they are well coloured. (Alternatively, place them in an uncovered roasting pan in a pre-heated oven at 220°C/425°F/gas 7.) Pour off any fat, add the water and bring to the boil slowly. Skim off the scum as it forms on the surface. Simmer for 2 hours. Keep skimming until the scum stops forming.

Heat the remaining oil in a large frying pan (skillet) and cook the chopped vegetables until brown, turning frequently. Add them to the stock with the tomatoes, thyme and bay leaf. Simmer, uncovered, for another 1 hour.

Strain the stock through a sieve (strainer) lined with paper towels or muslin (cheesecloth). As the stock cools, any fat will rise to the top. To remove the fat while the stock is still warm, carefully draw a sheet of paper towel across the surface. Alternatively, let the stock get cold and carefully lift off the fat layer that sets on the surface — this is sometimes called defatting.

Makes about 2.5 litres/4½ pints/2¼ quarts

Average servings of soups. *As a general guide, for a starter serve 250 ml/8 fl oz/1 cup; as a main meal, 450 mls/¾ pint/16 fl oz/2 cups.*

Chicken Stock

SUGGESTED INGREDIENTS

1.75 kg/3¾ lb to 2 kg/4½lb chicken
   carcasses and bones or chicken pieces
2.5 litres/4½ pints/2¼ quarts cold water
6 black peppercorns
12 parsley sprigs

Few sprigs of thyme, optional
2 white onions, skin remaining, roughly chopped
2 celery sticks, chopped
2 carrots, roughly chopped

Place the chicken in a large saucepan with the other ingredients and bring to the boil slowly. Skim and simmer gently, uncovered, for 3 hours. Strain and remove the fat (p. 48).

Makes about 2 litres/3½ pints/2¼ quarts

Fish Stock

SUGGESTED INGREDIENTS

500 g/18 oz fish bones, heads and
trimmings, washed
900 ml/1½ pints/1 quart cold water
1 onion, roughly chopped

1 celery stick, roughly chopped
6 white peppercorns
1 mace blade or a good pinch of ground nutmeg
1 teaspoon salt

Place the fish pieces and the water in a saucepan and bring to the boil. Skim off any discoloured froth from the top (p. 11). Add remaining ingredients and simmer gently, uncovered, for a further 30 minutes. If cooked longer, the stock becomes bitter. Strain (p. 11) and discard the bones and vegetables. Use the stock within two days or freeze it in sealed containers.
Makes about 750 ml/1¼ pints/3 cups.

French Onion Soup

This soup is very well known—a real winter favourite. Make your own beef stock, or use a canned broth if time is limited.

60 g/2 oz/¼ cup butter
1 tablespoon oil
675 g/1½ lb onions, thinly sliced
1 tablespoon salt
2 tablespoons flour
2 litres/3½ pints/2¼ quarts beef stock
  (p. 11), boiling

125 ml/4 fl oz/½ cup dry white wine or vermouth
Pepper
12 thick French bread slices
125 g/4 oz/½ cup butter, melted
2–3 tablespoons brandy
200 g/7 oz/1¾ cups Gruyère or mature Cheddar
  cheese, coarsely grated

Melt the butter in a large saucepan. Add the oil and onions and cook, uncovered, over a low heat for 20 minutes, stirring occasionally, until a rich golden colour. Be careful not to burn the onions. Sprinkle in the salt and flour. Stir over a moderate heat for 3 minutes. Remove from the heat and stir in the boiling stock gradually. Add the wine or vermouth and season with pepper. Return to the heat, cover and simmer for 30–40 minutes.

Brush the bread slices on both sides with the melted butter. Place in a single layer in a shallow baking dish and bake in a preheated oven at 160°C/325°F/gas 3 for 20 minutes, or until lightly brown and dried out.

Just before serving the soup, adjust the seasonings and stir in the brandy. Ladle or pour the soup into soup bowls. Top each serving with two bread slices and sprinkle over the cheese. Alternatively, sprinkle the cheese over the bread slices in the baking dish and bake for a further 5 minutes or until the cheese melts.
Serves 6

French Onion Soup with Garnish—the best chef's advise cooking the onions slowly to ensure a sweet, succulent flavour.

Chicken Corn Noodle Soup

Chinese in style, this hot soup is based on chicken stock and creamed corn. The cornflour mixture clarifies the soup, and the addition of whisked egg white and milk creates fine noodles.

3 chicken breasts, skin removed
400 g/14 oz can creamed corn
1.25 litres/2¼ pints/5¼ cups chicken
   stock (p. 11)
Salt and pepper
2 egg whites

1 tablespoon milk
1 tablespoon cornflour (cornstarch) blended with
   2 tablespoons water
6–8 spinach leaves, stalks cut away, torn coarsely
3 spring onions (scallions), finely chopped
   diagonally

Cut the chicken into long, thin strips. Place the creamed corn and chicken stock in a large saucepan and bring to the boil. Add the chicken strips, reduce the heat and simmer gently for 5 minutes. Season with salt and pepper. Whisk the egg whites until frothy but not forming peaks, then whisk in the milk and leave to stand while you continue the recipe. Stir the cornflour mixture into the soup, stirring continuously until boiling. Add the spinach leaves and spring onions, then pour in the egg white and milk mixture. Stir the soup a few times to allow the egg white to coagulate and form noodle-like strands on the surface of the soup. Serve immediately.

Serves 8

Ravioli Brodo di Manzo

A soup with origins in Northern Italy, brodo di manzo is usually served with a little pasta, rice or croûtons added. For something a little more substantial, ravioli have been used in this variation. Small tortellini are another option.

2 litres/3½ pints/2¼ quarts beef stock (p. 11)
125 ml/4 fl oz/½ cup dry white wine or vermouth
2 tablespoons tomato paste
1 bay leaf

250 g/9 oz/24–30 small ravioli
Pepper
Parmesan cheese, grated

Place the stock, wine or vermouth, tomato paste and bay leaf in a large saucepan. Bring to the boil, stirring continuously. In a separate saucepan cook the ravioli in plenty of boiling water, a few at a time, over a moderate heat for 8–10 minutes or until they rise to the top of the pan. Lift them out with a slotted spoon and place some in each of the bowls. Remove the bay leaf from the soup, season the soup lightly with pepper and ladle it into the bowls. Serve the Parmesan separately.

Serves 6

Ravioli and Tortellini in Soup

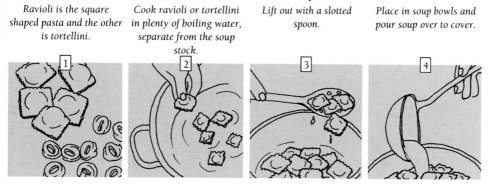

1. Ravioli is the square shaped pasta and the other is tortellini.

2. Cook ravioli or tortellini in plenty of boiling water, separate from the soup stock.

3. Lift out with a slotted spoon.

4. Place in soup bowls and pour soup over to cover.

Consommé

This clear, concentrated broth will stimulate your appetite at the beginning of any meal.
There are many classic French garnishes – a few simple ones are suggested here for you to try.

1.4 litres/2½ pints/6¼ cups cold brown stock
2 egg whites, lightly beaten
2 eggshells

200 g/7 oz/1¾ cups finely minced (ground) beef
2–3 tablespoons dry sherry or Madeira

Place the stock in a clean saucepan with the egg whites, shells and beef. Bring to the boil slowly, whisking occasionally with a fork or wire whisk. Allow the liquid to rise in the pan as it reaches boiling point, then draw the pan aside. Boil once more, taking care not to break the crust that forms on the top. Lower the heat and simmer very gently for 30 minutes. Strain through a sieve (strainer) lined with muslin (cheesecloth), holding back the crust with a slotted spoon until all the liquid has left the pan. The consommé should be clear. If not, strain again through the residue in the lined sieve into a clean bowl. Return to the heat, add the sherry or Madeira and the garnish of your choice.
Serves 6

Consommé. *A consommé is made by further simmering good beef or chicken stock to concentrate flavour and produce a crystal-clear liquid by clarification. Consommés can be served hot or chilled. Often you will find that a well-made consommé will set into a natural light jelly which can make an appealing starter course to a summer meal. There are a few tips you should know about before you begin clarifying a good base stock: Ensure that your utensils are spotlessly clean. The use of egg white and eggshells aids in bringing together the solid particles to form a white crust which, once formed, must not be broken. Dry sherry or Madeira improves the flavour and is added just before serving. Lean minced (ground) meat adds extra rich flavour and assists in clarifying the fine solids in the stock.*

Garnishes

Add finely sliced (julienne) strips of carrot or leek; cook in the soup for 5 minutes. Add 1 tablespoon of cooked long-grain rice per serving. Add finely chopped herbs or snipped chives. Beat 1 egg in a bowl, whisk in 2 tablespoons of plain (all purpose) flour until smooth. Season with salt and pepper. Press through a fine sieve (strainer) over the simmering soup.

Watercress Vegetable Soup

All the vegetables may be prepared ahead and the soup assembled just before serving.
Remember, it is important to keep the stock simmering gently between pouring or ladling it over each serving.

2 carrots	½ cucumber, halved lengthwise
1 leek, washed, (below)	60 g/2 oz small mushrooms
2 celery sticks	36 watercress leaves
1 mignonette lettuce	2 litres/3½ pints/2 quarts chicken stock, simmering
1 tomato	Extra sprigs of watercress, to garnish

Cut the carrots and leek into very fine julienne strips. Cut the celery into thin diagonal slices. Wash the lettuce, choose six outside dark green leaves and six lighter inside leaves, roll them up and shred them finely. Peel the tomato, remove the seeds and cut the flesh into small cubes (p. 37). Wash the cucumber, scoop out the seeds with a teaspoon and cut the flesh into tiny cubes. Cut the mushrooms into thin slices.

Drop the carrot, leek and celery into a saucepan of boiling water, cook for 3–4 minutes until tender yet still crisp. Drain and refresh in cold water. Place equal amounts of shredded lettuce and watercress in six large soup bowls, and divide the cooked vegetables between each. Add the tomato, cucumber and mushrooms. When required, pour or ladle some chicken stock into the bowls. Garnish with the extra watercress.

Serves 6

To clean leeks. *Cut off and discard any dark green leaves (they are too tough and can be bitter). If using the leek whole, cut it down the middle to about 2.5 cm/1 inch from the root end. Wash it very thoroughly under cold water, spreading the layers gently, making sure all grit is washed out. If leeks are to be chopped or sliced, it is easiest to cut them before washing*

Watercress Vegetable Soup. This delicately flavoured soup is enhanced if you keep the stock simmering gently as you ladle out the servings.

Julienne Vegetables

Cut carrot into fine slices.	*Stack carrot slices, then cut into pieces the size of a matchstick.*	*Finely slice leeks lengthwise, then cut into pieces the size of matchsticks.*	*Snip the chives with kitchen scissors.*

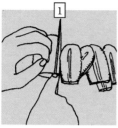
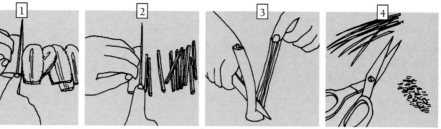

Lemon Chicken Soup

This light soup makes its own simple stock.
The addition of lemon juice and mint adds a freshness similar to the Greek avgolemono soup.

575 g/1¼ lb chicken thighs or breasts,
   skin removed
1 large onion, finely chopped
1 teaspoon salt
2 litres/3½ pints/2½ quarts water

125 g/4 oz/½ cup short-grain rice
4 tablespoons lemon juice
6 tablespoons chopped mint
Thin lemon slices

Put the chicken pieces, onion and salt in a very large saucepan. Add the water and bring it slowly to the boil. Simmer for about 30 minutes or until the chicken is tender. Lift the chicken pieces on to a plate and leave to cool. Add the rice to the saucepan and simmer for 20 minutes. Meanwhile, remove the chicken flesh from the bones and cut it into thin strips, using a small, sharp knife. Add the strips of chicken to the soup with the lemon juice and mint. Reheat gently and serve each bowl of soup with 1 or 2 lemon slices.
Serves 6

Pastry caps. *Pour warm soup into individual ovenproof bowls. Using ready-prepared pastry sheets, cut out circles of pastry to just fit over each bowl. Brush a little water around the rim of the bowl and place the pastry circle on the bowl; pinch or press down the edges to secure the pastry. Cut out shapes — for example, stars, leaves, and so on — from pastry scraps if you want to add extra interest; brush them with water and place them on the cap. Sit the bowls on baking sheets and bake in a preheated oven at 200°C/400°F/gas 6 for 12 minutes or until the pastry is golden brown.*

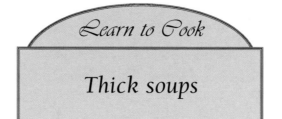

Learn to Cook

Thick soups

Among the cuisines of the world there is a wonderful collection of thick and hearty soups — chowders, minestrones, Mediterranean fish stews and lentil potages, to mention a few. These well-known and popular soups are very comforting, almost meals in themselves, with many relying on slow simmering to develop their characteristic flavours. Some of the recipes are traditional, but some shortcuts have been introduced to speed up the cooking processes for those with busy lifestyles. Crusty breads, piping hot muffins, savoury toasted snacks, cornbread or tossed salads and fruit are all you need to add for a nourishing meal.

Preparation of ingredients for Minestrone Genovese Soup (p. 23). Here is an opportunity to be creative with a selection of your own vegetable favourites—but don't forget the basil!

Spicy Coconut Peanut Soup

Unusual in flavour, this spicy hot soup is a style of 'laska' originating from Thailand.
Chinese cabbage and curry paste can usually be found in Oriental stores or large supermarkets; however, if you
can't get them, use ¼ small firm cabbage and all-purpose curry powder.

1 tablespoon peanut oil
1 onion, finely chopped
4 garlic cloves, chopped
1½ tablespoons grated fresh root ginger
1 teaspoon ground turmeric
1 teaspoon ground coriander
1 teaspoon curry paste
250 g/9 oz potatoes, peeled

750 ml/1¼ pints/3 cups chicken stock (p. 11)
250 ml/8 fl oz/1 cup coconut milk
¼ Chinese cabbage, finely shredded
3 tablespoons crunchy peanut butter
2 tablespoons soy sauce
Juice of 1 lime or lemon
1 teaspoon sugar
Spring onions (scallions), finely chopped

Heat the oil in a large saucepan. Add the onion, garlic and ginger and sauté for about 1 minute.
Add the turmeric, coriander, curry paste and potato. Cook, stirring continuously, for 1–2
minutes. Add the stock and coconut milk. Simmer for 10–12 minutes or until the potato is tender.
Add the cabbage, bring back to the boil, reduce the heat and simmer for 2 minutes only. Remove
from the heat. Mix a little of the soup into the peanut butter, soy sauce, citrus juice and sugar.
Stir this into the soup. Adjust seasonings to taste. Garnish with the spring onions.
Serves 4–6

Preparing Asian Vegetables

| Finely shred Chinese cabbage with a large, sharp knife. | Slice the garlic clove horizontally then vertically. Holding it together firmly, cut crosswise into dice. | Cut a piece of a ginger root and peel it. | Grate it. A Chinese bamboo ginger grater is shown here. |

 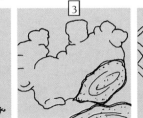 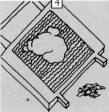

Red Lentil Soup

This soup, with it's distinct Middle Eastern flavour, can be made with water; however, if you use a beef
or chicken stock, it will be richer and tastier. Any variety of lentil - red, green, yellow or brown - can be used.
The red lentils are best if time is at a premium, because their cooking time is shorter than the other varieties.

3 tablespoons oil
1 large onion, chopped
1 celery stick with leaves, chopped
375 g/13 oz/2 cups red lentils, washed if necessary
2 litres/3½ pints/2¼ quarts water, or chicken
  or beef stock (p. 11)

Salt and pepper
Juice of ½–1 lemon
1 teaspoon ground cumin
Garlic croûtons (this page)

Heat the oil in a saucepan. Add the onion and celery and sauté for 6 minutes, until the onion softens. Add the lentils and water or stock and bring to the boil. Skim away any froth. Reduce the heat and simmer for 30–45 minutes depending on the quality and age of the lentils. If the lentils have not disintegrated, put the soup in a food processor or blender in batches and blend to a coarse purée. Return to a clean saucepan, bring to the boil again, adding a little water if a thinner, lighter soup is required, or simmer a little longer to reduce and thicken.

Season with salt, pepper, lemon juice and cumin. Simmer for a further 4–5 minutes. Serve with garlic croûtons.

Serves 6

To Crush Garlic

Place unpeeled garlic on board and crush with the flat of a heavy knife.

Peel the garlic.

Sprinkle with salt.

Finely chop the garlic.

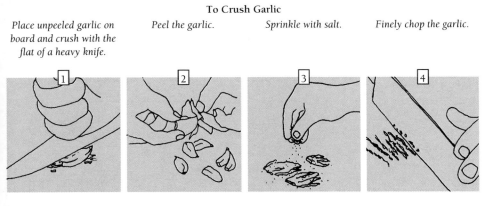

Garlic croûtons. *Crush a clove of garlic (this page) and combine it with 4 tablespoons of oil. Remove the crusts from 4 slices of bread, brush lightly with garlic oil and cut into small cubes. Heat a frying pan (skillet), add 2 teaspoons of oil and swirl the pan to coat the base. Add half the bread cubes and cook over a low heat, tossing the croûtons with an egg slice until they are golden brown and crisp (keep the heat low and be patient; too high a heat will cause croûtons to burn). Place them on paper towels. Repeat with the remaining bread cubes. To make plain croûtons, simply leave out the garlic.*

Minestrone Genovese with Pistou

A wonderfully warming, appetizing favourite to which you can add your own vegetable combination.
The pistou is a Provencal version of pesto, an Italian sauce for pasta; here the basil herb flavours the soup.

1 litre/1¾ pints/4¼ cups chicken stock (p. 11)
400 g/14 oz can peeled tomatoes chopped
500 ml/17 fl oz/generous 2 cups dry white wine
2 onions, diced
3 carrots, diced
1 turnip, diced
2 celery sticks, sliced
2 red peppers (capsicums, bell peppers), diced
1 large courgette (baby marrow, zucchini), sliced
125 g/4 oz/¾ cup elbow macaroni, or penne pasta
450 g/1 lb can red kidney beans, drained

½ teaspoon ground turmeric
Salt and pepper
Parmesan cheese shavings, to garnish

PISTOU
1 bunch (about 40 leaves) basil
3 garlic cloves, crushed
60 g/2 oz/½ cup Parmesan cheese, finely grated
4 tablespoons olive oil
Salt and pepper

Place the stock, tomatoes, wine, onions, carrots, turnip, celery and peppers in a large saucepan. Bring to the boil, reduce the heat and simmer for 20 minutes. Add the remaining soup ingredients, simmer for a further 40 minutes, stirring regularly, until the vegetables are tender. Place the basil, garlic and Parmesan in a food processor or blender. Blend until finely chopped. While the motor is running, gradually add the olive oil through the top of the machine until a paste is formed. Season with salt and pepper. Serve in large soup bowls. Stir in 1 tablespoon of pistou into each bowl.
Serves 8–10

Chopping an Onion

Peel onion and cut in two, leaving the root intact to hold each side together.

Make vertical slice down the length of the onion.

Make horizontal slices down the depth.

The onion half is still intact at root end. Slice crosswise to obtain dice.

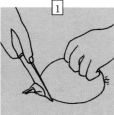
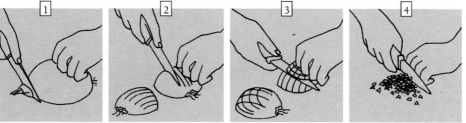

Minestrone Genovese with Pistou—a hearty traditional soup from the heart of Italy, full of nourishing fresh vegetables and highlighted with pistou.

Risi e Bisi

Rice and fresh peas combine in this famous soup from northern Italy. Venetians insist that the best time to prepare this soup is in spring, when the peas are young, fresh and tender. As an alternative, frozen peas can be used.

30 g/1 oz/2 tablespoons butter
1 lean bacon rasher (slice), rind removed
1 small onion, grated
250 g/9 oz/1½ cups shelled fresh or frozen peas
1 litre/1¾ pints/4¼ cups chicken stock (p. 11)

300 g/11 oz/1¾ cups short-grain rice
60 g/2 oz/½ cup Parmesan cheese, finely grated
Salt and pepper
Chopped parsley, to garnish

Melt the butter in a saucepan. Add the bacon and onion and sauté over a low heat for 5 minutes, until the onion is lightly coloured.

Add the peas and a few tablespoons of the stock. Cover and simmer for 20 minutes for fresh and 10–15 minutes for frozen peas. Add the rice and half the remaining stock. Bring back to the boil, lower the heat, cover and simmer for 15 minutes until the rice is tender.

Add the Parmesan and season with salt and pepper. Stir in more stock if desired; the soup should be fairly thick. Sprinkle over parsley, remove from the heat and stand for 1 minute before serving.
Serves 4

Lamb Shank Broth

A nourishing soup made with water. The vegetables and lamb shanks create a light, meaty flavour.

30 g/1 oz/2 tablespoons (or ¼ stick) butter
1 large onion, sliced
4 lamb shanks
3 litres/5¼ pints/3½ quarts water
90 g/3 oz/½ cup barley
3 celery sticks, sliced

2 large carrots, sliced
2 large parsnips, diced
1 teaspoon salt
Pepper
Chopped parsley, to garnish

Melt the butter in a large saucepan. Add the onion and cook over a low heat for 10 minutes. Add the shanks, water, barley, celery, carrots and parsnips. Season with salt and pepper. Cover and simmer for 1½–2 hours. Remove the lamb shanks and chop the meat. Return the meat to the soup and discard the bones. Adjust salt and pepper if necessary.

Serve sprinkled with parsley and accompanied with wholemeal crusty bread rolls.
Serves 8

Overleaf: Seafood Stew (p. 27) is made mouthwatering and substantial by an extensive variety of local fish and seafoods. This exotic concoction can be prepared easily in a very short time.

Corn Bacon Chowder

American in origin, the chowder is a chunky potato-and-milk-based soup with many variations. Plain salty biscuits (crackers) are the preferred accompaniment.

15 g/½ oz/1 tablespoon butter
4 bacon rashers (slices), rinds and fat
  removed, chopped
1 onion, thinly sliced
500 g/18 oz potatoes, cut into 2.5 cm/1 inch cubes
1 litre/1¾ pints/4¼ cups boiling water

400 g/14 oz can corn kernels or creamed corn
400 ml/14 fl oz/1¾ cups milk
½ teaspoon thyme
Salt and pepper
Worcestershire sauce

Melt the butter in a large saucepan. Add the bacon and onion and sauté until the onion is soft and bacon is slightly crisp. Add the potatoes and water. Simmer, uncovered, for 10–15 minutes until the potatoes are tender but not mushy. Stir in the corn, milk and thyme, return to the boil and season with salt, pepper and Worcestershire sauce.

Serves 6

Variation: Omit the bacon and add, with the milk, 200 g/9 oz of drained canned crabmeat and 250 g/9 oz of chopped shelled prawns (shrimp), or flaked smoked cod or haddock. (To prepare the fish, place it in a frying pan [skillet], cover with water and simmer 10–15 minutes, then lift it out, remove any bones and flake it into pieces.)

Preparing Prawns (Shrimp)

Take off the head.   *Break away the shell, leaving the tail intact.*   *Cut along the back.*   *Extract the intestine with a skewer. Wash well.*

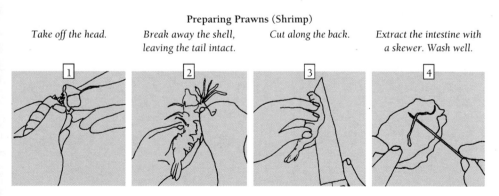

Seafood Stew

Fish soups sound exotic, but they are easily prepared in a minimum amount of time, 40 minutes or so at the maximum. There are many variations. The well-known bouillabaisse of France and the burride of Spain, to mention two, are more like stews, where local fish and seafood are simmered carefully in a good fish stock base. The choice of fish and seafood depend on locality, cost and availability, these ingredients are flexible. You can simply use a selection of fish or concentrate on a single seafood such as mussels or scallops.

2 tablespoons oil
2 leeks, white section only, thinly sliced (p. 16)
2–3 garlic cloves, crushed
2 litres/3½ pints/2¼ quarts fish stock (p. 12),
    strained
400 g/14 oz can whole peeled tomatoes
1 teaspoon thyme
2 teaspoons paprika
1 teaspoon sweet chilli sauce

1 tablespoon tomato paste
1 kg/2¼ lb firm white fish fillets, cut into
    large portions
500 g/18 oz green prawns (shrimp), shelled
750 g/1¾ lb mussels, scrubbed
250 g/9 oz scallops, washed and trimmed
Salt and pepper
Chopped parsley and snipped chives, to garnish

Heat the oil in a large saucepan. Add the leeks and garlic and sauté over a low heat for 5 minutes. Add the fish stock, tomatoes, thyme, paprika, chilli sauce and tomato paste. Bring to the boil, reduce the heat and simmer for 10 minutes. Add the fish, prawns and mussels, cover and simmer gently until the fish becomes firm and white and the mussels open. Add the scallops and cook for 2–3 minutes only. Season generously with salt and pepper.

Arrange some fish and seafood in wide-based soup bowls, ladle over the hot stock, and sprinkle generously with parsley and chives. Serve with garlic bread.
Serves 8

Cabbage Soup with Cheese Dumplings

60 g/2 oz/¼ cup butter
2 small leeks, finely chopped (p. 16)
½ cabbage, finely chopped
250 g/9 oz meaty bacon bones
1 tablespoon flour
2 litres/3½ pints/2 quarts chicken stock (p. 11)
1 teaspoon salt
Pepper
½ teaspoon caraway seeds
1 tablespoon vinegar

DUMPLINGS
90 g/3 oz/¾ cup self-raising (self-rising) flour
90 g/3 oz/¾ cup mature Cheddar cheese,
  finely grated
1 egg, beaten
1 tablespoon milk, optional
1 tablespoon chopped parsley
Salt and pepper
Chopped parsley, to garnish

Melt the butter in a large saucepan. Add the leeks and sauté over low heat for 5 minutes. Add the cabbage, bacon bones and flour. Stir well. Add the chicken stock, salt, pepper, caraway seeds and vinegar. Bring to the boil, reduce the heat and simmer for 1 hour.

Meanwhile, place the dumpling ingredients into a bowl and mix them together to make a firm dough. Take small portions of the dough and, with wet fingers, roll them into 18 walnut-sized balls. Leave to stand until required.

Remove the bacon bones from the soup and cut away any meat from the bones. Return the meat to the soup, adjust seasonings and add an extra cup of stock if necessary. Bring the soup back to the boil and add the dumplings one at a time. Reduce the heat and simmer for 10 minutes until the dumplings have doubled in size.

Serves 6

Below: Preparation of ingredients for Cabbage Soup with Cheese Dumplings. Left: The Germans relish dumplings in their soups and you'll relish this robust combination of bacon, cabbage and cheese dumplings.

Cold Soups

Bright and subtle colours of tomatoes, melons, cucumbers, and cooked vegetables, when puréed and chilled, add an elegance to any summer meal. While some soups are specifically designed to be eaten cold, there are soups that are normally served hot, such as Mulligatawny Simmer (p. 40) or Sunset Cream (p. 37), which are excellent when lightly chilled, though they need less cream when they are served cold. A spoonful of crème fraiche, plain yoghurt or a few ice cubes, garnishes such as tiny florets of raw cauliflower, a few shreds of Parma ham (prosciutto), a spoonful of crab meat or fresh cucumber balls can add another dimension to cold soups.

Tomato Pepper Ice

This is a simpler version of the well-known Gazpacho Andaluz and one designed to be made from readily available canned tomatoes and juice. It is not only refreshing and delicious but also decorative. The garnishes may be stirred into the soup either before being served or by those about to enjoy this thick and crunchy salad-style soup.

2 white onions, roughly chopped
2 large green peppers (capsicums, bell peppers)
    seeded and roughly chopped
2 cucumbers, peeled, seeded and chopped
2 400 g/14 oz cans whole peeled tomatoes
750 ml/1¼ pints/3 cups canned tomato juice

125 ml/4 fl oz/½ cup to 200 ml/7 fl oz/¾ cup
    lemon juice
Salt and cayenne pepper
Ice cubes
Tiny stoned (pitted) olives (p. 30), to garnish, optional
Garlic Toast (p. 21), to serve

Place half the onions, peppers and cucumbers in a food processor or blender. Blend until finely chopped. Add the tomatoes and blend again. Pour the mixture into a bowl and stir in the tomato juice and lemon juice. Season with salt if required and a dash of cayenne pepper. Chill thoroughly.

    Finely chop the remaining vegetables separately and place them in small bowls for garnish. Chill until required. Place two or three ice cubes in each soup bowl; ladle or pour over the soup. Offer the prepared garnishes separately and serve with garlic croûtons.
Serves 8

> **To stone (pit) olives.** *With a small sharp knife make a cut across the top of the olive through to the stone (pit). Keeping the blade on the stone, cut round the whole olive lengthwise. Twist the two sides against each other to separate. Using the tip of the knife, release the stone gently.*

Preparation of Borsch (p. 32)—the secret of the Borsch soup is the sweet and sour combination of lemon and beetroot, offset by the finishing touches of sour cream, chives or caviar.

Vichyssoise

This classic soup originated in America but was developed by a French chef, Louis Diat, at the Ritz Carlton in New York. Basically it is a puréed potato and leek soup, which can also be served hot.

60 g/2 oz/¼ cup butter
4 leeks, finely sliced, including some green
 tops (p. 21)
Salt and pepper
4 potatoes, cut into dice

1.4 litres/2½ pints/6¼ cups chicken stock (p. 11)
475 ml/16 fl oz/2 cups milk, hot
250 ml/8 fl oz/1 cup double (heavy) cream
Snipped chives, to garnish

Melt the butter in a large saucepan. Add the leeks and sauté over a low heat until soft but not brown. Season with a little salt and pepper. Add the potatoes, stir in the stock, cover and simmer for about 30 minutes or until the potato is tender. Stir in the hot milk. Leave to stand until cool.

Pour or ladle the soup in two or three batches into a food processor or blender and purée until smooth. Pour the vichyssoise into a bowl and chill until required. Before serving, stir in the cream. Sprinkle chives over each serving and accompany with small cucumber sandwiches.
Serves 6-8

Piquant to the taste, colourful to the eye and filling to the stomach, Borsch has been a great favourite in Russia for generations.

Borsch

A Russian soup that is well worth the effort of making. The sweet-sourness of lemon and beetroot adds to the flavour, with soured cream, chives or caviar adding the finishing touch. You can also serve this soup hot. Crusty rye bread makes it a hearty meal.

750 g/1¾ lb fresh beetroot
1 large onion, finely chopped
1 celery stick, finely chopped
½ carrot, coarsely grated
400 ml/14 fl oz can beef consommé or 1 litre/
   1¾ pints/4¼ cups beef stock (p. 11)
1 stalk each parsley and dill if available
3 cloves

Sugar, salt and pepper
2–3 tablespoons lemon juice

GARNISH
Soured cream or plain yoghurt
Spring onions (scallions) or chives, finely chopped
Black and red caviar

Peel and coarsely grate two of the beetroots. Place the grated beetroot in a saucepan with the other vegetables. Add the beef consommé, made up as directed on the can, or beef stock, and the parsley, dill and cloves. Bring to the boil and simmer for 30 minutes. Strain through a fine sieve (strainer) and discard the solids. Stir in some sugar and lemon juice to taste, season with salt and pepper. Peel and coarsely grate the remaining beetroot; add it to the soup. Chill thoroughly to allow the flavours to infuse. Serve with a spoonful of soured cream or yoghurt, a sprinkling of spring onion or chives and a teaspoonful of caviar.
Serves 4

Guacamole Chill

A delicious avocado soup with a Mexican flavour of chilli and coriander (cilantro). If buttermilk is not available, substitute 250 ml/8 oz/1 cup of single (light) cream and an equal quantity of soured cream. Since avocado flesh darkens quickly on contact with air, work quickly or brush it with lemon juice or vinegar to prevent discoloration.

2 large ripe avocados
500 ml/17 fl oz/2 generous cups buttermilk
500 ml/17 fl oz/2 generous cups chicken stock
   (p. 11)
2 tablespoons lemon juice

2 tablespoons chopped coriander leaves (cilantro)
   or 2 teaspoons ground coriander
1–2 tablespoons mild chilli sauce
1 small white onion, finely chopped, to garnish
1 tomato, peeled and finely chopped, to garnish
Coriander (cilantro) leaves, to garnish

Cut one of the avocados in half, remove the stone (pit), peel away the skin and chop the flesh roughly (p. 34). Place it in a food processor or blender and purée to a creamy pulp. Add the buttermilk and chicken stock and blend again until combined and smooth. Blend in the lemon juice and coriander. Pour the soup into a bowl. Season with chilli sauce. Cover tightly with clingfilm (plastic wrap) to exclude air and chill for 1 hour, or longer if time permits.

Seed and peel the remaining avocado as above and cut the flesh into small dice. Stir them into the soup and adjust the seasoning. Serve a spoonful of onion and tomato on top of each serving and scatter over a few coriander leaves.
Serves 6

Preparing Avocadoes

Cut the avocado in half.   *Remove the stone and peel away the skin.*   *Slice avocado roughly.*   *Cut into dice and blend to creamy pulp in food processor.*

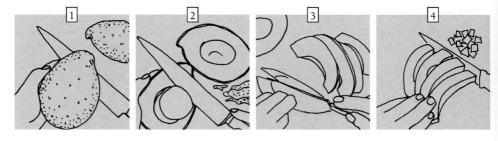

Iced Curry Fruits

2 cooking apples, cored and roughly chopped
1 banana, chopped
125 g/4 oz pawpaw (papaya), peeled, seeded and chopped
4 spring onions (scallions), finely chopped
425 ml/14½ fl oz can tomato juice
250 ml/8 fl oz/1 cup chicken stock (p. 11) or canned broth

½ teaspoon curry powder
Salt and pepper
250 ml/8 fl oz/ 1 cup double (heavy) cream
3 tablespoons desiccated (shredded) coconut
1 cooking apple, peeled and coarsely grated or chopped
Cooked strips of poppadum (below)

Place the apples, banana, pawpaw and spring onions in a food processor or blender and process until smooth. Blend in the tomato juice, stock and curry powder. Pour into a large jug or bowl, adjust seasonings and leave to chill for several hours.

Place the cream in a bowl, beat until soft peaks form, and then fold in the coconut and grated apple. Leave to chill. Serve the soup with a spoonful of cream mixture and poppadum strips.
Serves 6

To cook poppadums. *Heat 450 ml/¾ pint/2 cups of oil in a high-sided frying pan (skillet) or medium-sized saucepan, until hot. Add 1 poppadum; it will quickly puff up and become golden. Remove it from the oil immediately and drain it on a paper towel. Repeat with the remaining poppadums. To microwave, place 2 poppadums directly on the carousel, cook on High (100%) power, in 2-second spurts, turning over to crisp both sides. For poppadum strips, cut the uncooked poppadums into strips of various widths and cook as above.*

Iced Curry Fruits. A luscious medley of fruits and flavours comprise this light, curry-based fruit soup. And guess what? No cooking!

Cream Soups

This diverse category of soups appeals because any vegetable may be used. The staple potato, leek, onion and carrot or the more interesting fresh asparagus, spinach, peppers, peas, lettuce and watercress can be easily transformed into informal combinations.

Basically, the vegetables are simmered in water or light stock and usually puréed. Some need a binder or liaison which thickens the soup liquid so that the puréed ingredients remain in suspension rather than separate. The simplest liaisons are starches — rice, couscous, grated potato, tiny pasta shapes, to mention a few. Other cream soups, usually called veloutés, rely on a butter and flour roux or beaten egg yolks combined with cream, arrowroot or other cold liquid. When they are beaten into and heated with the soup, it will thicken slightly.

Single (light), double (heavy) or soured creams or crème fraiche are interchangeable last-minute additions, being swirled into the purées as part of a garnish. They give that final richness of flavour and smoothness that is characteristic of this extensive soup category.

Above: Preparation of egg liaison for Cream of Pea and Lettuce Soup. The delicate touch is achieved when the egg yolk and cream combination is quickly mixed with the purée and then poured back into the saucepan. Left: The finished soup ready to be eaten.

Cream of Pea and Lettuce

Both lettuce and peas provide a delicate light flavour when puréed and thickened with an egg liaison. You can also chill this soup for a hot summer's day.

30 g/1 oz/2 tablespoons butter
1 large onion, chopped
500 g/18 oz/3 cups shelled or frozen peas
1 red eating apple, peeled and cut into cubes
½ large iceberg lettuce or 1 butter lettuce,
    finely sliced
1.5 litres/2¾ pints/7 cups chicken stock (p. 11)
    or water

Salt, pepper and nutmeg
2 egg yolks
125 ml/4 fl oz/½ cup single (light) cream
Fried croûtons (p. 38)
Mustard and cress or chopped mint, to garnish

Melt the butter in a saucepan. Add the onion and sauté for 3 minutes or until soft. Add the peas and stir continuously until shiny and green. Add the apple, lettuce and stock. Bring to the boil, reduce the heat and simmer until the peas are tender — 15–20 minutes if fresh or 10–12 minutes if frozen. Purée the soup (p. 42). Season with salt, pepper and nutmeg.

Mix the egg yolks and cream together in a bowl. Quickly stir in about 250 ml/8 fl oz/1 cup of the purée to combine, then pour the mixture back into the saucepan. Stir over a low heat until the soup begins to boil. Adjust the seasoning. Serve immediately, scattered with croûtons, mustard and cress or mint.

Serves 6-8

Fried bread croûte. *Cut a circle out of a piece of sliced bread, preferably toasting thickness, with a pastry cutter. Heat about 2 cm/¾ inch of oil in a frying pan (skillet). When hot, fry the bread, turning it over during the cooking, until golden brown. Drain on paper towels.*

Garlic bread. *Cut a small loaf of French or Italian bread into thickish slices. Spread the cut surfaces with garlic butter. Reassemble the loaf and wrap it in foil. Bake in a preheated oven at 190°C/375°F/gas 5 for 20 minutes, open the foil and bake for a further 5 minutes, or until crisp. Serve immediately.*

Cauliflower Soup Gratin

The cheese gratin topping on this simple vegetable soup is optional. If you prefer, simply garnish with almond flakes or slivers fried in a pan with a little butter until golden and add some snipped chives for colour.

1 cauliflower
1 litre/1¾ pints/4¼ cups chicken stock (p. 11)
150 ml/¼ pint/⅔ cup milk or single (light) cream
30 g/1 oz/2 tablespoons butter
Salt and pepper
¼ teaspoon nutmeg

1–2 egg yolks
125 g/4 oz/1 cup Gruyère or Cheddar cheese, grated
60 g/2 oz/½ cup plain dried breadcrumbs
Chopped parsley to garnish

Remove the outside leaves and the thick central stalk from the cauliflower. Cut off the florets — halve them if large — and the smallest leaves. Cook them in boiling salted water until tender. Drain and purée until medium fine (p. 42).

Place the cauliflower purée back in the saucepan, add the stock and bring to the boil slowly. Stir in the milk or cream, butter and seasonings. Beat the egg yolks with a little extra cold milk or water in a bowl. Quickly stir in about 250 ml/8 fl oz/1 cup of hot soup to combine, then return the egg mixture to the saucepan. Stir over a low heat until the soup just begins to boil.

Combine the cheese and breadcrumbs in a bowl. Pour or ladle soup into four ovenproof 250 ml/8 fl oz/1 cup soup bowls and place them on a baking sheet. Sprinkle the cheese mixture evenly over each. Place under a moderate grill (broiler) until the cheese melts. Garnish with parsley and serve immediately.

Serves 4

Garlic butter. *Beat 125 g/4 oz/½ cup of butter until soft and creamy. Crush 1–2 cloves of garlic (p. 00), and mix into the butter. For herb butter, cream the butter with 2 tablespoons of finely chopped herbs such as parsley, basil or thyme, or a combination of herbs.*

Sunset Cream

Tomatoes, although available all the year, are not always at their peak of sweetness and ripeness, so an alternative is to use about the same weight of canned, whole peeled tomatoes and a little less water. A spoonful or two of tomato paste may be added for that additional rich, refreshing flavour. This delicious soup can also be eaten chilled.

30 g/1 oz/2 tablespoons butter
2 onions, finely chopped
2 tablespoons flour, sifted
1 kg/2¼ lb ripe, juicy tomatoes, peeled (p. 37)
   and finely chopped
1 teaspoon salt
2 teaspoons sugar

¼–½ teaspoon cracked peppercorns
¼ teaspoon sage, basil or oregano
1 bay leaf
1.15 litres/2 pints/5 cups water
Tomato paste, optional
Single (light) cream, to garnish
Chopped parsley, to garnish

Melt the butter in a large saucepan and cook the onions for 5 minutes, stirring regularly, until soft. Stir in the flour and cook for 3 minutes. Add the tomatoes, salt, sugar, pepper, choice of herb and bay leaf. Bring to the boil, cover and simmer for 15 minutes. Add the water and simmer for a further 15 minutes. Remove the bay leaf. Purée the soup (p. 42), return it to the saucepan, and bring it back to the boil. Adjust the seasonings, adding 1–2 tablespoons of tomato paste if necessary. Serve with a swirl of cream and parsley.
Serves 6

Orange Sunset Cream.
Peel an orange, cut the peel (not the pith) into fine strips and cook in boiling water for 1 minute. Drain and leave to stand. Squeeze the juice and add it to the soup purée. Adjust seasonings. Serve with a swirl of cream, orange strips and sprigs of mint.

Peeling Tomatoes

Cut a small cross on each tomato.

Put tomatoes in a bowl and pour boiling water over them.

Peel the skin away from the cross.

Chop tomatoes finely by slicing, then dicing.

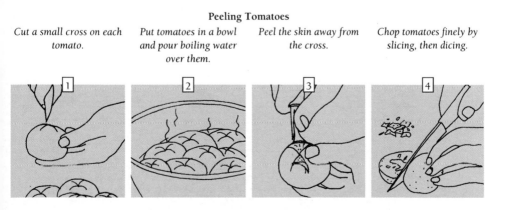

Mulligatawny Simmer

This thick vegetable version of the traditional Indian soup can vary in its distinctive flavour depending on the type of curry seasoning used – mild or hot curry powder, paste or a home-made combination you enjoy.

60 g/2 oz/¼ cup butter
2 onions, finely chopped
2 teaspoons curry powder
2 celery sticks, chopped
2 red eating apples, cored and thinly sliced
1 small turnip, chopped
2 tablespoons flour
1.4 litres/2½ pints/6¼ cups water

1 tablespoon lemon juice
100 g/3½ oz/½ cup long-grain rice
4 small courgettes (baby marrows, zucchini),
  thinly sliced
Salt and pepper
250 ml/8 fl oz/1 cup plain yoghurt
3 tablespoons desiccated (shredded) coconut
Cooked poppadums (p. 34)

Melt the butter in a large saucepan. Add the onion and curry powder and cook slowly for 5 minutes. Add the celery, half the apples and the turnip. Add the flour and cook for 1 minute, stirring continuously. Stir in the water. Bring to the boil and simmer for 20 minutes.

Add the lemon juice and rice. Stir until boiling again and simmer for 15 minutes. Add the remaining apple slices and the courgettes and simmer for a further 10 minutes or until just tender. Adjust seasonings if necessary.

Combine the yoghurt and coconut and serve with the soup and poppadums.
Serves 8

Right: Mulligatawny Simmer is spicy and distinctive in flavour, thick in texture, mild or hot according to your taste—and definitely to be served with cooked poppadums. Below: Preparation of roux for Mulligatawny Simmer.

Almond Velvet

Rice is simmered with leeks and ground almonds to add thickness to this light cream soup. It is also ideal served chilled with grated orange rind.

4 leeks, white section only, sliced (p. 16)
60 g/2 oz/¼ cup butter
1.5 litres/2¾ pints/7 cups chicken stock (p. 11)
300 g/11 oz/3 cups ground almonds

3 tablespoons short-grain rice
300 ml/½ pint/1¼ cups single (light) cream
Snipped chives or sprigs of watercress

Place the sliced leeks in a colander (perforated strainer) and rinse thoroughly in cold water to remove any grit. Melt the butter in a saucepan and cook the leeks over a low heat, stirring regularly, for 15 minutes or until soft. Add the stock, almonds and rice. Cover and simmer for 30 minutes. Cool slightly and purée until very smooth (p. 42). Rinse the saucepan, return the leek purée and stir in the cream. Reheat the soup until it just begins to boil. Serve immediately with chives or watercress.

Serves 6

Purée Soups

Purée soups make a wholesome variation to the roux or egg-liaison, cream-soup category. They are prepared from almost any root or green vegetable, lentil or pulse. The vegetables are usually cooked gently in butter or oil without colouring, simmered in well-flavoured chicken stock, puréed, and finished with cream or milk for added flavour and texture. This is the traditional method for purée soups. There is also a new style designed for you if you are health conscious or find you have the end of the week's vegetables in the refrigerator. Simply cook the vegetables in stock with seasonings, purée, and serve without the cream or milk. For casual dining or everyday meals, these purées should not be too thick — unless you prefer them that way — but light in texture and easy to pour into warm bowls.

Red Pepper Soup

Creole in style, this aromatic simple purée requires unblemished sweet peppers; the cream is an optional addition. Add a dash of finely chopped fresh chilli or paste for added spiciness. You will also enjoy this excellent soup chilled, served over a few ice cubes with wedges of lime or lemon.

2 tablespoons oil
1 garlic clove
2 red peppers (capsicums, bell peppers), cut
    into dice
1 brown onion, roughly chopped
1 carrot, roughly chopped
2 celery sticks, sliced
1 kg/2¼ lb ripe tomatoes, peeled (p. 37)
Pinch of saffron or ground turmeric, optional

2 tablespoons short-grain rice
750 ml/1¼ pints/3 cups chicken stock (p. 11)
1 tablespoon tomato paste
½ teaspoon basil
Salt and pepper
GARNISH
Double (heavy) cream, optional
Red pepper (capsicum, bell pepper), finely chopped
Sprigs of herbs

Heat the oil in a saucepan, add the garlic, peppers and onion and cook for 2 minutes. Add the carrot, celery, tomatoes and saffron or turmeric, if using, and cook for a further 2 minutes. Stir in the rice. Cover and cook gently for 5 minutes. Add the stock; stir in the tomato paste and basil. Cover and simmer over a low heat for about 1 hour. Season with salt and pepper. Purée the soup (p. 42). Return the purée to the saucepan and reheat, stirring regularly until just boiling. Adjust the seasonings and serve with cream, if using, chopped peppers and herbs.
Serves 4

Preparation of vegetables for Sweet Potato and Spinach Duo (p. 45) —a handy hint to thin this 'duo' is to use either extra stock or cream.

Herb ice cubes. *Finely chop herbs (parsley, chives, basil) in a food processor. Place 2 teaspoons in each cavity of an ice-cube tray, and fill with cold water. Freeze. Add herb ice cubes to hot broths, stirring to dissolve, or to summer soups just before serving.*

Sweet Potato and Spinach Duo

Both these unusual dinner party soups can be enjoyed individually and will serve four generously. You can substitute pumpkin and watercress and still use the same method. This versatile duo combination may need to be thinned if they are too thick; use either extra stock or cream – it is your choice.

SWEET POTATO SOUP
675 g/1½ lb sweet potatoes, coarsely chopped
4 carrots, coarsely chopped
1 litre/1¾ pints/4¼ cups chicken stock (p. 11)
5 cm/2 inch cinnamon stick
Salt and pepper

SPINACH SOUP
30 g/1 oz/2 tablespoons butter

1 onion, chopped
1 bunch spinach, washed, trimmed and chopped
   coarsely
1 potato, chopped
1 litre/1¾ pints/4¼ cups chicken stock
2 strips orange peel without white pith
Salt and pepper
Nutmeg

Place the sweet potatoes, carrots, stock and cinnamon in a large saucepan. Bring to the boil, cover and simmer for 30 minutes or until the vegetables are tender. Discard the cinnamon. Purée the soup (p. 42). Season with salt and pepper. Return the purée to the saucepan and leave to stand.

Melt the butter in a large saucepan and cook the onion over a low heat for 5 minutes. Add the spinach, potato, stock and orange peel. Season with salt, pepper and nutmeg. Cover and simmer for 25 minutes. Discard the orange peel and purée the soup (p. 42). Return the purée to the saucepan.

Reheat both soups, stirring regularly over a low heat until just boiling. Holding a pan of soup is each hand, or using two ladles, carefully pour the soups together into shallow bowls so that they naturally meet in the centre. Serve with thin bread sticks or small savoury muffins.
Serves 6

Toasting almonds. *Spread blanched almonds on a baking sheet. Roast in a preheated oven at 180°C/350°F/gas 4 for 4 minutes, remove the baking sheet from the oven, shake it or turn the almonds over with a fork, then return them to the oven for a further 3–4 minutes or until golden. Remove the almonds from the hot baking sheet immediately, or they will continue cooking.*

Sweet Potato and Spinach Duo—a soup fit for a dinner party, this delicious combination is also highly nutritious.

Broccoli Potage

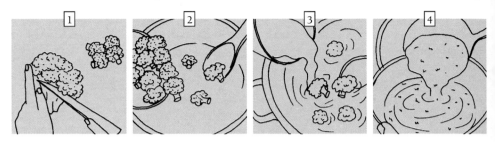

| Cut the broccoli into florets. | Add broccoli to melted butter and leave to sweat for 10 minutes. | Add stock and seasoning and simmer until broccoli is tender. | Purée the soup in the food processor and put back over the heat to warm up. |

Broccoli Potage

This basic formula can apply to any vegetable combination of your choice.

60 g/2 oz/¼ cup butter
750 g/1 ¾ lb broccoli, cut into florets with
    some stem
500 ml/17 fl oz/generous 2 cups chicken stock (p. 11)
½ teaspoon nutmeg

Salt and pepper
125 ml/4 fl oz/½ cup single (light) or double
    (heavy) cream
Toasted almond flakes, to garnish (p. 45)

Melt the butter in a saucepan, add the broccoli and cook, stirring regularly, over a medium heat for 10 minutes. Add the stock and seasonings and simmer for 20 minutes or until the broccoli is tender. Remove a few cooked florets and reserve to use as garnish.

    Empty the saucepan into a colander (perforated strainer) over a bowl. Ladle some of the broccoli and stock into a food processor or blender and purée by using the pulsing switch, or turning the machine off every second or two, until the contents are blended to a medium or fine purée, but not so fine as to lose all its texture. Pour this back into the saucepan and continue the puréeing until all the broccoli and stock are used. Stir in the choice of cream and reheat, stirring continuously, without boiling. Serve with toasted almond flakes and the reserved broccoli florets. *Serves 4–6*

Variations
Asparagus: Replace the broccoli with 750 g/1¾ lb young asparagus, ends snapped off and stems cut into 12 mm/½ inch dice, leaving 5 cm/2 inches of tips, and 1 onion, finely chopped.
Mushroom: Use 750 g/1¾ lb mushrooms, wiped with a damp cloth and sliced, and ½ teaspoon dried oregano or ground coriander. Remove some of the cooked mushrooms before adding the stock and reserve for garnish.

Roast Pumpkin Soup with Saffron Threads

This delicious soup has a unique nutty sweet flavour as a result of roasting the whole pumpkin up to a day in advance. If time is short, simply simmer peeled pumpkin chunks in the stock for a basic purée (p. 48).

1.5 kg/3¼ lb whole pumpkin
475 ml/16 fl oz/2 cups chicken stock (p. 11)
125 ml/4 fl oz/½ cup single (light) cream
125 ml/4 fl oz/½ cup milk

1 teaspoon brown sugar
1–2 teaspoons lemon juice
Salt and pepper
A few saffron threads, to garnish

Place the whole pumpkin on a baking sheet and cook in a preheated oven at 200°C/400°F/gas 6 for 1 hour or until tender when pierced with a fork. Allow to cool for 30 minutes.

Cut the pumpkin in half top to bottom with a sharp knife. Remove and discard the seeds. Scoop the soft pulp from the shell and place it in a food processor or blender. Process to a smooth purée (p. 42). Add the stock, cream, milk, brown sugar and lemon juice and process again until well combined. Pour the purée into a saucepan and reheat gently. Season with salt and pepper.

When served, float saffron threads carefully on top to garnish.

Serves 4

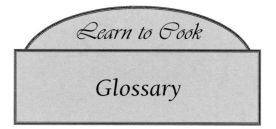

Learn to Cook

Glossary

Blend Combine two or more ingredients together until smooth.

Binding Thickening a liquid by adding starch, eggs or gelatine.

Blanch Immerse foods briefly in boiling water, to make them easier to peel or to partially cook them or remove too strong a taste. Always followed by refreshing — the foods are then plunged into cold water.

Bouquet garni A bunch of herbs, usually parsley, thyme and a bay leaf, with peppercorns and a small stick of celery, tied together and used to flavour soups and casseroles. Remove before serving.

Chill Place in the refrigerator until cool/cold.

Chop Cut into very small pieces with a sharp knife.

Clarify Clear stock or broth by adding beaten egg whites and crushed egg shells and bringing to the boil; the stock is cooled and strained before using.

Cool Allow to stand at room temperature until no longer warm to the touch.

Croûtons Small toasted or fried pieces of bread.

Defat Remove fat from a liquid by chilling so that the fat rises to the surface and sets, or by blotting the surface lightly with sheets of paper towel.

Dice Small, even cubes.

Florets The small flowering stems that make up the head of broccoli or cauliflower. Mostly cooked with little or no stalk.

Garnish Decorate dish with a small savoury ingredient — for example fresh herbs — before serving.

Gratin A dish sprinkled with breadcrumbs and/or cheese and browned in the oven or under a grill (broiler).

Julienne Even-sized thin sticks of vegetables or fruit. Thickness varies depending on dish and use.

Joint Cut poultry or game into serving pieces by dividing at the joint.

Liaison Thickening agent for soup — a mixture of egg yolks and cream, among other things.

Peel The skin of citrus fruits, also called rind; zest usually refers to the thin outer skin.

Poach Cook gently (simmer) in enough hot liquid to cover, using care to retain shape of food.

Potage A French word for soup.

Purée Cooked and sieved foods, usually fruit or vegetables, made by putting through a sieve (strainer), food processor or food mill.

Reducing Boiling away the quantity of liquid for a specified time or by a specified amount; this concentrates flavours or consistency.

Roux A mixture of melted butter and flour cooked over a low heat with milk, stock, or wine added, which is the base of many sauces and soups.

Saffron The dried or ground stigmas of the *Crocus sativus*. It is the rarest and most expensive of spices.

Sauté Cook or brown in a small amount of oil or butter.

Shred Cut in fine lengths.

Skim Remove froth or scum from the top of simmering liquid, using a big spoon or spoon-shaped sieve.

Simmer Cook liquid slowly, just below boiling. Small bubbles appear, but the liquid is practically motionless; it looks as though it is shivering.

Whisk Beat at high speed with a fork or kitchen whisk using a circular motion.